In This Moment

In This Moment

Making the Most of
Your Senior Years

Antonia Albany

Santa Rosa, California

Albany Books
2777 Yulupa Avenue, #333
Santa Rosa, California 95405-8584

Printed in the United States of America
Published Sepember 2015

Library of Congress Control Number:
ISBN:. 8978-0-9966424-0-8

Design by Randall Friesen

This book is dedicated to my dad.

He never got to enjoy many of his senior years.
He'd be happy I'm thoroughly enjoying mine.

Acknowledgments

I wish to thank Randall Friesen for his expertise in editing and adapting material that appeared previously in various locations including my blog. He painstakingly compiled years of my writings on all things about aging and was able to make the information eminently more readable and coherent. Tasks that were insurmountable to me were second nature for him.

I also enormously appreciate my friend, Norma Miller, and my husband, Rod Sverko, for reading and rereading drafts and for providing invaluable input.

Thanks also to the large cadre of friends who continue to inspire me and who represent the graceful and grateful aging spoken of in these chapters.

Contents

Introduction

Fifteen years ago as I edged toward senior-dom I began looking at print and online resources on aging. I found lots of information about senior living programs, assisted living housing and myriad geriatric products to aid my passage through the last part of my life. I also found zillions of cartoons and, what I found to be, slightly offensive stories and jokes about seniors—their sex lives, lack of agility and mental equity, as well as their pervasive forgetfulness. None of this material was particularly relevant or entertaining. What I read did not describe me or my life, nor the lives of my friends, or even remotely the circumstances of life as I know it.

The entirety of what aging has encompassed for me so far is presented here in thoughts and musings, which include friendships, family, spirituality, pets, self-awareness and improvement, and the power of each one of us as individuals making the most of the rest of our lives regardless of our circumstances. I hope this book illuminates your path and creates more joy in your life process.

We're on this planet for whatever time we have left. Let's make the most of it!

In This Moment

The Best Is Yet to Come

Society has suggested we not trust anyone over thirty. And even though people over thirty make up the largest segment of the population, advertisers often ignore this significant audience.

The senior population has historically been pushed to the side and told, "It's all downhill now, baby! You've already lived your best life, had the most fun, amassed your greatest wealth, enjoyed the most rewards life has to offer and had the best sex you'll ever experience." However, this is changing as advertisers see the financial potential in the older crowd. More and more we hear comments like, "Sixty is the new forty" and "Eighty is the new fifty."

If I ever doubted that the best is yet to come, all I have to do is think about Louise Hay. This metaphysical teacher and motivational author is well into her eighties and still going strong. Hay was born into a poor and abusive family and ran away from home at fourteen. She dropped out of school and married at fifteen and was pregnant a year later. She gave up the baby at birth, at which point her husband left her for another woman.

In the late 1970s, Hay found that she had cervical cancer. She refused conventional treatment and began a regime of forgiveness coupled with therapy, nutrition, and reflexology. She claimed that she rid herself of cancer by this treatment. While many would have lamented that "the best" was nowhere in sight, she saw the positive and turned things around. She studied New Thought authors and spiritual teachers, including Ernest Holmes, who taught that positive thinking could heal the body.

Louise Hay has written nearly thirty books on affirmations and the power of positive thinking. In 1984 she established Hay House Publishing and has worked with Deepak Chopra, Ester and Jerry Hicks, Oprah Winfrey and Wayne Dyer. Her bestseller, *Heal Your Body*, has sold more than thirty-five million copies around the world in over thirty languages. She loves to sing, dance, paint and sculpt, activities she didn't even start until well into her seventies. She is a living example that the best is *always* yet to come.

Well-known people who remind us that life can be very fun and rewarding are great examples for us, yet I find it particularly inspiring to have friends who epitomize a positive attitude regardless of age. My friend Barbara was one of those people.

I met Barbara when she volunteered in my unit at the Sheriff's Department. She was seventy-five. We quickly became friends, and when her project ended, she went to another department where she organized a large library. Eventually the library was named after her. We had lots of fun together playing cards, going out, and traveling abroad.

When Barbara was seventy-nine she met an eighty-year-old British man on a cruise. They corresponded and visited each other for a year, and a year later they married and she moved to England. They had a lovely time enjoying each other before she passed away a few years later. I attended her wedding in England, and one day we took the train to Paris for lunch. The last time I saw her she was wearing a bright red beret and a brilliant smile.

I bet you know someone like this. They may not be famous or rich, and they may be a lot older than you. What do they have that makes them open and receptive to the best when it appears? If I were to guess, I'd say a significant factor is their attitude. We all have our bad days, but in general, these people are upbeat and positive. They're certain that there are good times ahead, regardless of their age, finances or marital status. They're the ones who see the glass as half full, that rainy days are opportunities to stay in and read, and that the actions of others don't dictate their happiness.

Metaphysicians believe that like attracts like, and we believe the best is now and forever. I aspire to this way of life and enjoy working on it. I'm grateful I've got outstanding role models to keep me knowing the best is yet to come.

Gratitude
Your Most Valuable Ally

It's legal, non-fattening and laudable. It costs nothing. It remains quiet when ignored but blossoms when revealed. It can be your most powerful weapon and your best friend. Quite simply, I'm referring to gratitude, the state of being appreciative or thankful.

Millions of words have been written about the practice of incorporating gratitude into your life. The nature of its accessibility and ease of use makes it, to some, not as worthy as a gadget that costs a lot to obtain and maintain. And because it's not tangible, it's sometimes easy to forget.

Indeed, I could tell you about the found money, free services and gifts, an unexpected trip to Paris and other things I've received from practicing gratitude, but that's not where its true value lies.

Gratitude is my most valuable ally because it provides me the greatest amount of joy and peace. Nothing I can purchase or whip up in the kitchen brings me the clarity and overall well-being of feeling gratitude. I can always count on it to bring me joy and a sense of satisfaction. It is constantly available for my use, and, like meditation, the more I use it, the more I receive from it.

Practicing gratitude is easy, and my usage has increased over the years. I've found several methods that enhance the results of incorporating gratitude into my daily life. My foremost method for tapping into gratitude is openness.

A few years ago I broke my wrist while training dogs for the Humane Society, where I had been volunteering after recently retiring from a rewarding, high-powered job. It was a bad break and I was in the hospital for three days. To make matters worse, my sister, who was only three years older than me, had recently died. I was miserable, and I wondered, "Why me?"

When I got home from the hospital I was virtually helpless. With one hand functional, I couldn't drive or cook, nor could I do much work on the computer. I even needed help showering and dressing for the day, and I was to remain in this condition for seven weeks.

At the end of week one, it dawned on me that there was not a thing I could do but be available to this experience. I closed my eyes, opened my arms and, standing in a brilliant ray of streaming sunshine in my living room, declared, "Okay, God, I'm open and receptive to whatever I'm meant to get out of this experience." Instantly I became grateful that my broken arm had made my life settle down so that I could take time to reevaluate my future. My life clearly shifted to a better place from that point forward.

Based on this traumatic experience, I learned the value of starting and ending each day with an homage to gratitude. Some people find that a gratitude journal works well to reinforce the routine and allows them to look back from year to year to observe how their gratefulness may have changed.

My daily gratitude routine is somewhat less formal, but it works for me. When I wake in the morning, I swing my feet over the edge of the bed, but before they touch the floor, I raise my arms overhead and say a simple "Thank you."

My evening routine adjusts my body and mind to the end of the day. I give thanks for the richness of my life and offer specific praise for any highlights. Many nights I only have enough energy to groan a delicious, "I love my bed," as I slide between the sheets. There are no rules; whatever works in the moment is perfect.

With a wider breadth of life experience, senior citizens have an advantageous opportunity to practice and benefit from gratitude. Our perspective on life is broader and less hectic and we have more time to reflect on what works and what doesn't. We've "been there, done that" when it comes to acquiring material possessions. Now it's about acknowledging those practices that have consistently brightened our life, lightened our load, and made us more in harmony with the universe.

I feel the power of a potent tool in gratitude, and I'm inspired to share it with others. Give it a try!

How to Be Wealthy

Based on the title of this chapter, you may think I'm about to present a lengthy, detailed lecture on ways to gather, invest and save money. After all, money is the way society deems us as wealthy. Isn't wealth the "true measure of a man"? But money is merely one measure of wealth.

Sometimes investors purchase currencies from other countries to round out their portfolios and stave off any economic shifts that threaten their financial strategy. Dollars in whatever form—cash, stocks, IOUs, foreign currencies—are good things. The more the merrier!

But you can be an extremely wealthy person without money.

My mother measured her wealth in terms of vodka and house slippers. After she passed away, we found six gallons of the former and thirty pairs of the latter in her home. If stashes like hers determine true wealth, then mine is mayonnaise. I've always got several jars in my pantry and can get a little twitchy when I'm down to just one or two.

I also adore paper, particularly expensive Asian paper. Though I can rant and rave when the bill for my car registration comes, I've got reams of paper that cost me a fortune and that I will probably never do anything with except look at. It's what you value that makes you feel wealthy.

I also have many books, and they make me feel wealthy. I have an entire wall in my office lined with shelves filled with books. I have sold a ton of used books too, and the $3.50 I've gotten for 10 boxes of books is real mad money for me. I'm clearly not talking dollars-and-cents logic here.

Now that I've covered the "stuff" of wealth, let's

look at a less tangible commodity.

Friendship is a way of measuring and exemplifying wealth. At parties where I'm being feted, I feel wealthy. Nothing exemplifies the bounty of a life more than the number and character of friends one can count on to be there for you. Granted, this group would be greatly reduced if I needed help moving instead of throwing a party for them. Seriously though, I've always felt friendly people are an unquantifiable measure of one's wealth.

Dollars and cents come and go, so it is beneficial to measure wealth in other ways. It's also good to look at different options available for wealth so we don't feel so stuck during a bad economy. True wealth doesn't involve saving or hoarding.

What is your true wealth? What makes you feel whole and able to stand strong in harsh economic and emotional times?

What Kind of Friend Are You?

I'm not a perfect friend, but I'm a better friend than I used to be. Being a friend takes work. Though this seems counterintuitive, it is true for me. Some people make friendship seem so effortless, but it doesn't come naturally for me. I have to assess and perfect my friendship skills constantly.

I never had any formal friendship training as a child, except turn the other cheek, do unto others, etc. Instead, I was taught to be competitive with others. The message in our household was, "Don't let them get ahead of you. Always watch your back." As a result, I was convinced that everyone was out to take advantage of me or make me look bad. I always had to be on my guard, which makes building long-lasting friendships a difficult task at best. Since my dad was in the military and our family moved frequently, it was easy to develop the façade of friendship without doing the work of developing long-lasting relationships.

Throughout my childhood, I had two unconditional friends. The first was my cocker spaniel, Sparky, and the second was my collection of books. Neither of these "friends" would criticize nor judge me. I spent more time with my dog and my books than with human beings.

Another speed bump in my friendship journey was that I was encouraged to seek out friendships with men but not women. I was in my twenties before I realized that the other half of the population was worth befriending.

I'll never forget the first time I could say I loved a woman as a friend. I was surprised by the depth of feelings I had for this co-worker, whom I saw as a symbol of the value of female friends. My friend Christine was nurturing and kind and had no ulterior motive for getting close to me. She inspired me to see the people in my life through a different lens, and from her I learned to build female friendships. For the first time in my life I felt alive and worthy and not so suspicious of women around me.

I know there are other women who lacked early friendship development like I did because I've met many of them throughout my life, and we've compared notes about being guarded around other women and unsure of their sincerity.

This doesn't mean that I'm an expert friend and that people—both men and women—are clamoring to be on my speed dial. In fact, I've got a long way to go in perfecting my technique.

Last year I completely alienated a dear friend by not being honest with her about how I felt about the manner in which she behaved. Instead of saying I was feeling ill at ease with her conduct, I behaved rudely to her regarding a completely unrelated issue and hurt her feelings. I did this three times, and the last time I did it she never came back. My goal since then has been to repair this fissure, but only time will tell.

I'm surprised that this kind of thing happens to a senior citizen such as me. I truly thought I'd have figured out by now how friendships work and that I'd be basking in the glow of shared warm feelings for everyone in my close circle. There is, however, more than one important lesson to be learned here.

Friendships are not stagnant. There may be people in my life today who won't be here this time next year, not because of advancing age but because of something said or done that alters the tide and makes a space for different people in the future.

When I ask myself what kind of friend I am, I can now answer softly with a great deal of compassion for my foibles, "I'm the best kind of friend I know how to be today, and I will improve in the future."

Books and pets continue to rank right up there as the relationships I value, but all the great learning opportunities I receive from "people" friendships are just too juicy to pass up.

It's never too late.

Lighting the Way

Have you noticed, late at night when nature's call draws you out of the comfort of your warm and cozy bed yet again, there are few completely dark places anymore? Have you noticed the plethora of electronics lighting up the night? It used to be that you could easily break your neck in the middle of the night by running into a door left ajar or a slipper kicked out of its normal location.

"Pitch black" doesn't exist in my house anymore. I can see nearly everything in my house even when it's dark—really dark—outside. I can glimpse my black cat Kali stealthily traverse my bedroom at two a.m. and see her kitty toys scattered on the carpet in the living room. If I go outside in the middle of the night, my backyard patio is lighted by the nearby street lamps.

Even when the power goes out in my home, I have enough battery-operated electronic devices—smoke and carbon monoxide detectors, alarm clocks and cell phones—to illuminate the entire area below my loft. The only reason I need candles during a power outage is because I can't read by the red glow from the battery-operated digital clock next to my bed.

I have twenty-five indicator lights that radiate in my home at all times, day and night. Why are these tiny indicator lights always on? Do I really need all of them? I'm not sure if this lack of total darkness should comfort me or if I should consider this a waste of natural resources.

The brightening up of our nighttime hours has been a gradual process, perhaps starting with the small, red indicator lights of our telephone answering machines and our stoves with digital time displays. As I look around my house, I am aware that these lights are in the company of a dozen others I'm paying to keep aglow.

Maybe it's not that big of a financial deal, but it causes me to wonder how much further we're moving toward bright nights.

How many lights are on all the time in your house, and does this bother or comfort you?

Community Volunteering

I live in Santa Rosa, California, the county seat of Sonoma County, a 1,768 square-mile community just north of San Francisco. The population is just under 500,000.

As reported in our local paper, Sonoma County houses one of the largest volunteer populations in California. Nearly two out of every five adults in the county do some sort of volunteer work. The percentage of Sonoma County residents who donated time in 2010 outpaced all other Northern California communities surveyed that year. In addition, volunteer percentages of local residents significantly surpass the national average.

Though I was aware that I live in a community of volunteers, I was surprised to learn that these statistics were so impressive. I'm not sure why this part of the country is so generous with their time and talents. Perhaps it is because we have a large retired population, or at least one affluent enough to have the time and resources to volunteer.

Communities will always need volunteers, and this need will continue to grow as time goes on. In spite of attempts to fill positions with paid staff, many organizations financially rely on volunteers now more than ever. For instance, one of the largest hospitals in Santa Rosa has approximately 135 volunteers to staff the front desk, gift shop and emergency waiting room. These dedicated individuals, ranging in age from the late nineties, greet and guide stressed and ill clients to the places they need to be in the quickest way possible. These volunteers also interact with visitors and staff from other institutions and on occasion even with law enforcement personnel. Without the volunteers, maneuvering the hospital could be pretty frustrating. Often we look right through these volunteers and don't even notice them. People can be distracted and sometimes not at their best when needing their services.

Books are one of my most beloved things. When life sucks and people around me seem a bit crazy and non-supportive, I always have my glorious books. That's why I donate my time to Schools of Hope. The Schools of Hope volunteers work with first- and second-grade students in local elementary schools. Surprising as it sounds, many students this age don't have a firm grasp on reading, which prevents them from graduating later. The program currently serves approximately 700 students in twenty schools, and there are plans to increase the stable of volunteers from 400 to 800.

Senior citizens are not required to do volunteer work once we have retired, but it can actually make you feel better. When the inside of my house closes in and I find myself getting too much into my head, there's nothing like a precious seven-year-old to change my perspective. My tutee, Tyler, is a good reader and loves to show me how he has progressed from week to week. However, the walk with him to and from the classroom, when we talk about holiday festivities or weekend events, is sometimes worth the drive to the school in itself. How can a child help but flourish with such undivided attention from an adult?

Volunteering is where I can begin. Whether it is formulating policy for inmate programs in the county jail or successfully managing megabucks in taxpayer dollars, it is making a difference in the lives of those I work with, be they young and curious children or scared and dying patients.

The next time you find yourself watching yet another reality show on TV, remember you could be making a huge impact in your life as well as in the life of another by volunteering your time. If you are inclined, explore your local volunteer possibilities. Whether it takes a half hour a week or forty hours a week, it will change your life.

Is Christmas Just For Kids?

The first Christmas I remember as a child was when I was nine years old and my family was living in Japan. I still believed in Santa and had a long list of wants that year—a big-girl bicycle, a Madame Alexander doll, and majorette boots with tassels on the front.

On Christmas morning I was not disappointed. My sister and I, still in our pajamas, tried to restrain ourselves as we walked down the hall to the living room. The lights from the tree gave off a brilliant glow that lighted our way even though all other lights in the house were off. In the distance I heard the whir of my dad's Super

8 camera as he prepared to capture every look and gasp of glee. The living room was nearly impassible due to the bounty of presents for my sister and me. It was truly magical.

I don't remember another childhood Christmas that extravagant. It seems my Christmases veered abruptly from gluttonous gift orgies to the one when I nervously wondered what was in the tiny box from my boyfriend Ed. Hopefully it was a pearl ring. I had gotten him an awful gold-green sweater that made him look truly ill. In those days we didn't—or couldn't—afford to spend more than twenty dollars on each other.

Years later I would throw that pearl ring at Ed when I found out he wanted to go out with Heather, whom he eventually married. To this day, however, Ed and I remain friends and we often laugh about those early times. As a military brat who frequently moved, it is comforting to have a friend who has known me for over thirty years.

After the initial years of marriage to my first husband, Christmases focused on the meal and the guests. We loved our large kitchen in Bodega Bay with its windows steamed up from myriad foods cooking on our tiny range. The kitchen was big enough to hold a couch and a kitchen table, and our guests drank wine and played with the cats, who used the opportunity to run in and out through the sliding glass doors as often as our guests did.

With no children of our own, meals, family and friends were the focus of our Christmas activities. Art and I eventually separated, and soon after I was introduced into my second husband's extended family. After my father passed, my mother and sister would sometimes join us.

Many Christmases were spent driving to Oregon to be with Chuck's family. Christmas Day would find us on the road, where a McDonald's burger would substitute for the usual gourmet meals prepared at home. Though we lived in a converted barn without a lot of amenities, Chuck could barbecue anything and I could even make a delicious apple crisp in the Weber grill.

Christmas today is all about the grand kids. We now let others do the frenzied planning and preparing. We satisfy ourselves by contributing a dish or two and lending a hand to build a fire or distract a wee child who is melting down after an action filled day.

Invariably I remember that Christmas in Japan when I was nine: the wonderment, the excitement, and the sheer joy of being so blessed. I see a lot of that reflected in the faces of the kids today. The gifts I receive now are not found in the material things, the delicious food and drink, or even in knowing that my presence is welcomed and appreciated. The gifts I receive are the kind I get all year long. They may not be as exciting, but they never break and their batteries never run low.

A Fresh Start

January 1 is not so much about making resolutions—resolutions I usually keep for a week at the most. It's not about sincere yet vague goals to eat better or exercise more. It was that way in the past, but now that I'm a senior citizen, I'm no longer so naïve about such promises.

New Year's Day is about new beginnings. It is the first day of the rest of your life. Despite the sugary nature of that cliché, it does cause me to pause and wonder what the New Year will bring.

Throughout the month of December I often hear

people say something like, "The new year has got be better. It can't be any worse than this last one." Yet it seems we've been saying that for many years now! While this is a fairly negative outlook on the previous year, the sentiment is borne out of many years of publicized or personally experienced economic turmoil—joblessness, foreclosures, rollercoaster gas prices and general uncertainty.

January 1 is like the first day of spring in that it's a fresh start. A fresh start, whether large or small, is a good thing. It's an opportunity to take stock of your life. A fresh start is a gift. It offers us hope and welcomes us to incorporate new and better things into our lives.

New beginnings are blind to age and resistant to the economy. There are an unlimited number available to each and every one of us. What we do with them is our choice. We can talk about them with our friends and then ignore them if we want, which is like subscribing to *Martha Stewart* magazine and looking at the pictures but not making any pies.

Each moment is a fresh start, a new year, a Monday morning. Your gift bag filled with new beginnings is just as full today as it was yesterday, so go crazy. Try on some new habits, some new ways of doing things that might bring you a greater sense of well-being.

What if you resolve to do something differently but it doesn't happen? It doesn't matter! You will have another chance— a moment, a day, or another New Year later—to try it again if you really want it.

What are you looking for in the New Year? If it's change you seek, it's going to have to come from you, to be envisioned by you, created and developed by you, and be integrated into your life. You can't do the same thing and expect a different result.

So bring it on! Roll around in all the possibilities. And don't forget to have fun.

Kali

The way I feel about my cat, Kali, is fairly unreasonable and can make my close friends uncomfortable. My love for my cat is immense. I can just look at her and I burst into tears. Is this the way it is with children? I don't know; I never had any. How could I feel this manic level of care and devotion for a cat?

Several years ago my friend Robert and I were both in the market for pets. He wanted a dog and I wanted a cat. We visited every shelter and Humane Society in two counties. Each weekend we'd head out and see if any new pets might be out there waiting for us. We did

In This Moment

• *35* •

this for months but never found the right one. Then it happened.

One day Robert found his doggie, Princess, a white *bichon frise* mix, at the local pound. Two days later I found a cat named Ali, hidden in the back of a small room at the Humane Society. The moment I sat down on the floor, she boldly popped out of her cage and began rubbing against my thigh. That's when I noticed she had only three legs. Her rear flank was shaved where her left leg had recently been amputated.

She seemed starved for attention. Although somewhat shy about letting me get too close, she couldn't get enough of my thigh against her sweet face as she rubbed and purred against me. She had been attacked by a dog, with her leg hanging lifeless for several days before her owners brought her to the Humane Society because they couldn't afford the surgery. Only one year old, she was in good health despite this trauma, so the veterinarian just removed the dead limb.

I met Ali two weeks after that surgery, and from that first meeting I knew she was mine. I immediately made the necessary plans for her to come home with me the next day. The first thing I did was change her name. My spouse's ex-wife's name was Ali, so that just wouldn't work. I changed her name to Kali, which means "black" in India.

Kali can't survive in the outdoors with only three legs, so she is content to consider the inside of my home her entire world. She only succeeded once in dashing out the front door. She scooted around the outside of the house and ended up in a parking area, bawling loudly. I lured her back with wet cat food and scooped her up into my open arms. She and I both were trembling. Since that day, she's never again been interested in going outside. I could leave the front door wide open and she'd just sit and stare at it.

Even now she's quite skittish; she hates loud noises, like ice cubes rattling around in the ice tray, the sound of tinfoil being ripping off the roll, boisterous guests, doors opening or closing, or anything to do with plastic bags. I gladly tolerate this behavior from her because she's been through quite enough traumas in her life.

If I don't shower or put my makeup on, if I have a grumpy day with nothing good to say, if I get too busy and ignore her, or if I go on vacation and leave her for two weeks in the care of others, she's always loving to me. She holds no grudges and is always happy to curl up in my lap or lick my leg or reach out a tiny paw to my cheek when I cry.

I'd like to think I saved her, but when I look into her soft kitty eyes and feel she's seeing into my soul, I realize she saved me. She saved me from never having felt that level of love from an animal friend.

She must know I'm thinking about her right now because she just rubbed up against my leg as I was writing this. Then again, it is dinner time. Maybe that's all it is!

Anthropomorphize
It's More Than a Long Word

Anthropomorphize. I love that word, mostly because I know how to pronounce it. And because I'm an expert at it. I anthropomorphize all the time. People make fun of me because I anthropomorphize so much. Yet at the same time I can get irritated when I see someone else anthropomorphizing.

Webster defines *anthropomorphize* as "to attribute human form or personality to things not human." For example, when I leave my cat with a sitter while I go on vacation, I imagine that she (the cat, not the sitter!) is upset, angry and standoffish upon my return and that she's punishing me for leaving her for so long. I do most of my anthropomorphizing with my cat, Kali, but there are many examples of this trait.

One well-known illustration of anthropomorphism is in the story of Adam and Eve, where the serpent is given the ability to talk in order to tempt Eve to eat the forbidden fruit. Stories can be more appealing and less threatening if the characters are animals, as in *Peter Rabbit* or *Watership Down*. Dressing a pet in human clothes or other costumes may be an extreme form of anthropomorphism—cute, but sometimes creepy.

There is no way to know how many human emotions, if any, an animal may experience. Associating human traits to animals, in particular our pets, has been the subject of many research trials attempting to quantify the extent to which animals experience emotions such as anger or sadness.

I recently saw an experiment on television which dealt with the possibility of a pet feeling guilt. Maybe you've seen that look on a pet's face when they get caught shredding the toilet paper or sneaking food. This is how the test was conducted: A dog sits in an empty room. The dog's owner enters, places a treat on the floor and leaves. The dog just sits there. Soon another person comes in the room takes the treat and leaves the room. When the owner returns and scolds the dog, the dog looks guilty. The researchers concluded the dog was responding to scolding actions and voices, not necessarily the feeling of guilt.

But what about empathy? As I sit on the couch watching the movie "Terms of Endearment," Kali is in my lap. When I start to get weepy (as I do every time I watch this movie) Kali looks up at me and stretches her little paw out to touch my check. The look in her eyes tells me she's thinking, "Oh, mom, don't cry." I'm *sure* that's what she's thinking.

It's a good thing I know about anthropomorphism.

Ten Tips to Make
Senior Moments Happier

Retirement is all about relaxing and enjoying life more. It's time to quit sweating the small stuff and start appreciating the goodness all around us. We're done meeting deadlines, we're done raising families (hopefully), and we're done worrying about things we cannot control.

I'd like to offer my ten tips to keep in mind for this time of life. This list isn't stagnant. It represents a process of growth, expansion and introspection to improve the quality of our lives.

1. Stop worrying about getting older.

Time marches on. We can either go with the flow or fight it like a salmon swimming upstream. I can tell I'm fighting it when I see myself wearing age-inappropriate clothes or makeup to hide wrinkles and laugh lines.

Most people don't care so much about how we look or dress as we get older. They want us to be kind and gentle with them, to share our experiences and to listen. And we can do that. We've got the experience and the time.

2. Stop comparing yourself to others.

My mother used to remind me that there was always someone else better, smarter, and prettier than me, and at the same time there would always be people with much less than I had in all those departments. And I'll be darned if she hasn't been right all these years! We are each unique, and we each bring distinctive qualities to this life experience. This uniqueness allows us to relate to others, not to compete with them. Comparing ourselves to others is a huge waste of time.

3. Stop thinking you have plenty of time.

Buddha says, "The trouble is you think you have time." We may have many years of life ahead of us, or not. Who knows? Don't think, "Oh, I can start writing that book later" or "I have plenty of time to gather my family's ancestry information." Stop wasting time now, and begin treating each day as an opportunity to get closer to your goals.

4. Stop isolating yourself.

Many seniors live alone. We may be widowed or divorced and our kids are grown and gone. Sure, we have friends, and many of them are alone as well. It's easy to let two, three, or more days go by without reaching out to relatives and people who care about us. It can be easy to rely on social networking as our primary contact with people, however, there is no substitute for a hug or the direct gaze into the eyes of someone who will laugh with you, someone who will hold your hand and listen to the inane details of your day. This is important.

Call someone. Arrange to get together, even if it's super casual—without makeup, a fancy hair do, or any expensive fanfare.

5. Pay attention to gratitude.

Like attracts like. I'm a firm believer that gratitude expands the Universe and makes room for good things to enter. The greatness I've gotten in life has never come as a result of being skeptical or entitled. It's when I open myself to all that is available to me that goodness comes forth abundantly. And I am grateful.

6. Stop sitting on your butt.

Move the body, a little or a lot. When I find myself sitting for a long time—at my computer, in front of the TV, knitting or reading, in conversation with others—I feel gravity pulling everything down, settling into my tush and legs. As we age, it's important to keep things moving. The phrase "use it or lose it" is significant for seniors. Sometimes all I can do is a chair exercise, but my goal is to do more than just talk about moving my body.

7. Stop needing to be right.

In my forties, I always needed to be right; it was part of my job, or so I thought. Being liked as opposed to being right came as I matured.

Think about a time when someone was in your face barking out an explanation that showed their "correct" thought processes and actions. Did it feel like a human connection, or were you just a sounding board for their ego? Most people never ask for information or for someone else's input at all.

8. Stop trying to control everything.

Most of us want the world to rotate on our own axis. We're sure we know the best way to do things, and we're always expounding on those thoughts. At the same time, we see that the only real control we have is over ourselves and that anything other than that is a waste of time and energy. Letting go of a specific outcome is a good place to begin to let go of control. Be willing to be vulnerable. There are several ways to accomplish something, so why not let another person share their way with you?

9. Stop trying to change others.

Most of us want to be accepted and validated for being just the way we are. Trying to change others is a lesson in futility. It gives them the message, "You are *not* okay the way you are." Work on changing yourself, and let others be the unique and wonderful people they are.

10. *Stop allowing negative thoughts to invade this glorious time of life.*

Negative thoughts are time stealers. They rob you of being open to gratitude and all the wonderfully uplifting things in the Universe. Time spent in negativity brings more of it into your life. Joy and feelings of abundance will never come out of negativity. Positive change doesn't come out of criticism or negative emotions.

This is my list of helpful hints about growing old gracefully. You may have your own list, or at least could expand on this list significantly. This moment—now— is our time to have fun and make the most of what we have and our position in life.

When Bad Things Happen

School killings, deadly fires and acts of terrorism can make the world feel scary and dangerous. But if we focus on the idea that bad things happen, our lives will become fearful and not very fulfilling or joyous.

When the bombs exploded at the Boston marathon, I was surprised by my own feelings. For the first time that I can remember, I didn't immediately turn on the TV. Instead, I found myself become peaceful. It's definitely not that I didn't feel profoundly sad about the loss of lives and horrendous injuries. But I didn't want to stop everything else in the world and plug into the story. I didn't start talking to friends and conjecturing about the who and what. I didn't start that familiar tape in my head that says, "You should be scared. Bad things happen all the time, so you should be vigilant about what might happen in your town" or "Don't get too happy or else something bad will take away your joy."

I tend to be a sponge more than a filter. When I hear bad news, it doesn't simply register and then pass through me. It stops in my body, my mind, my soul, and I can't shake it off. I have to work hard to get enough information about the situation without getting so much that I can't function in the rest of my life.

I absorbed the main points of the Boston bombing through the succinct MSN headlines on my computer. After that, I ignored the news on TV or in the newspapers until President Obama gave a speech at the interfaith prayer service. I watched that. Then when it was over, I turned off the TV and only checked back after the perpetrators had been captured and a motive was presented. After that, I checked in with a friend who lives in Boston and made a donation to One Fund Boston. That was it. Life goes on for me. It helps no one if

I stay stuck in sorrow, angst and fear.

I know that the world is a good place, a safe place, an abundant place. Yes, bad things happen, but I'm not willing to let those things—either events of the past or those in a possible future—tarnish my certainly of the goodness that exists or interfere with the quality of my current actions. Staying sad and curtailing my activities because of sorrow in no way assists the victims or anyone else. Am I sad about what has happened? Yes, I am. But I'm not tossing that wet blanket of sorrow into the Universe to dampen the spirits of others.

How did I develop this calmness? It started when I began to focus on forgiveness in my life. Forgiveness is about letting go. There's a saying, "Forgiveness means giving up all hope for a better past." To me, letting go gives way to a calmer reaction to things that go wrong. I realize I have no control over scary events, but I can control how I respond to them.

I have identified five thoughts that work for me when dealing with tragedy in the world:

1. Don't try to pretend the terrible event didn't happen, but don't wallow in it either.

Avoid TV and newspaper articles that repeatedly speculate about the who, what and why. Avoid conversations with friends and family who want to wallow in the horrific nature of the event.

2. Check your worry levels.

Worry saps your energy and robs you of emotional stability, whether you are worried about the victims or about your own situation.

3. See if there is anything you can do to help.

Can you donate time, money or efforts? You can always pray. Once you have done what you can do, let go of the outcome of your contribution.

4. Visualize how you will respond.

How you respond will depend on the situation. If the event is local or within your family, you will respond differently than if it involved people you don't know far away. Either way, it's beyond your control. The best thing you can do is to remain calm and empathetic, but slightly detached. Being calm is the goal.

5. Focus on the positive.

Reaffirm the goodness in life by spending time in uplifting activities: family, pets, nature, crafts, music, books, etc.

There is no right or wrong way to handle catastrophe. This isn't a test that you either pass or fail. It is best to deal peacefully with whatever life throws at you. I'd rather show up in a tranquil mode, ready to do what I can, and then let go of all the rest.

Show Me the Basket

I have a magic basket. It is not a real wicker basket that is tangible. It is a visual aid I keep in my mind to hold solutions to problems, ways to cope with life, and fun activities when I am bored or need a reward. I am going to share with you what fun activities I retrieve from my virtual basket when I'm bored.

Before I retired, I thought long and hard about what I would do with my time once I didn't have to report for work every day or when I wasn't waking up in the middle of the night thinking about work problems or involved in the myriad tasks related to a work life, like getting clothes ready, making lunches, doing my hair, nails, etc. That adds up to a lot of time! So I wanted to be sure I had creative and fun activities to fill that time—not just to kill time, but to enjoy it.

When I go to my basket, I pick an item that bests suits my emotion. If I'm feeling bored between tasks, I may pick the "floss my teeth" item out of my basket. Sometimes just doing a simple thing, like flossing or reorganizing a junk drawer, can shift me from one emotion to another one, like feeling a sense of accomplishment or feeling cleaner or less like a procrastinator.

There are three locations I go to if I'm bored: the Dollar Store, a movie matinee, or the library. None of these places costs much, if anything, yet they can brighten up any day. All of these activities can be done alone or with a friend.

There are three Dollar Stores where I live; I get a total splurge at them with only $5. The last things I bought there were margarita glasses. They are fun, but since I only have margaritas maybe once a year, I'm getting them for a buck a piece, and if one breaks…oh well! Some of the best holiday knick-knacks and decorations can also be found there. And don't forget the stationary supplies, greeting cards, and plastic leftover food containers, which, at these prices, I can afford to send them home with guests and never get back. It is so much fun to stroll the aisles ferreting out little diamonds of cheap goods that, when mixed with my halfway decent stuff, will be just perfect!

The second of my special places is the movie house, specifically for matinees. I have my favorite theaters where the seats are comfortable, my feet don't stick to the floor and it's not run rampant with bored teenagers and raucous pre-teens. There are a couple of theaters that still make their popcorn fresh and in small batches, and I frequent these places the most. If you're a senior, you don't really have to go to the matinees to get a break on the price. I think the senior price, which is good all day, is still a quarter or so less than the matinee price. It's harder to get me out of the house after dinner, so I'm more likely to hit a matinee, even a late morning one.

Lastly, my favorite place to go is the library. The service provided by this county agency is a stupendous bargain. I've raved about the wonderful library system for years. I love nothing better than to read the *New York Times Book Review* and then reserve the books online, which will deliver them from any library in the system to your local library. The last request I made wound up coming from a college library hundreds of miles from my home. This inexpensive access thrills me to the core.

Some of these things may seem uninteresting and silly to you, but this is *my* basket after all. It's a good idea to think about things you can do to make yourself happy or entertained, whether you're retired or not.

The things in your basket will have nothing to do with anyone else's opinion; they belong to you. I guarantee that if you take a little time to create your own basket of things to do when you need something non-caloric, legal and within your budget, you'll find these items will be cemented as your version of life's little pleasures, as they have been for me.

How to Forgive

In a nationwide Gallup poll, ninety-four percent of Americans surveyed said they aspire to forgiveness, but only forty-eight percent said they actively took the steps to forgive. This represents a huge disconnect between what we say we want to do and what we actually do. Why is this? Do we see it as a weakness to be forgiving?

Recently I've been focused on the issue of forgiveness. This focus has given me the opportunity to examine more closely my beliefs about forgiveness and see what's working and not working for me.

One of the first things I discovered about myself is

that I forgave some people but not others.

My forgiveness practice has taught me that true forgiveness has nothing to do with others and everything to do with myself. While forgiveness benefits both giver and receiver, the one who benefits the most is the one who forgives. Yet the only true benefit I can get from forgiving is if I use it without judging who deserves it. Why is that?

As a metaphysician, I know what I give will be returned to me. If I give a loving feeling or thought of forgiveness to the Universe, that feeling will be returned to me. It doesn't matter if it is deserved by the recipient, returned by them or if they are even aware of my forgiveness. I'm not saying we should forgive someone and set ourselves up for possible pain again. Forgiveness is about the letting go part—letting go of the anger, pain, self-pity, angst, fear, etc. Letting go frees us, heals us and keeps us safe.

Scientific studies correlate the ability to forgive with less stress and better health, both of which have compelling implications for seniors. As we age, we could be accelerating the process by harboring the anger and resentment that accompanies the inability to forgive. Additional research has shown that the ability to forgive impacts happiness and the overall sense of well-being.

Once we see the value of forgiveness in its truest sense, how do we go about changing the way we think and act relative to it? How do we break the habit of judgment when choosing to forgive or not?

It starts with forgiving yourself. What do you need to forgive yourself for? Journaling works well for finding answers to this question, and an affirmation like "I forgive myself for judging others" is an example of what you might say to yourself if you're heading into old habits.

There is some good news about changing your forgiveness paradigm. First, you don't have to forget in order to forgive. And secondly, forgiveness can be taught with positive results. I made a spreadsheet for understanding my personal issues around forgiveness. It included the following questions I felt were important for me to address:

- Whom am I not forgiving?
- Why am I not forgiving them?

- What has not forgiving them cost me?
- What am I going to do to change my outlook?
  - prayer
  - meditation
  - affirmations
  - counseling

Others have used letter writing to work through the forgiving process, and many commit to journaling to examine the issues and make positive changes over time.

Changing your ability to forgive takes time, so don't be hard on yourself if you find the process takes longer than anticipated. Remember that you are forgiving not for "them" but for yourself.

Another method I use to change my way of thinking regarding forgiveness is to see the other person as an extension of myself. This may seem like a silly technique, but I look at my hand and see it attached to me, the same way the person I'm not forgiving could be. Would I be hateful and cruel to my hand? Would I cut it off because it made me mad or was disrespectful? Of course not. We are all one within this Universe, so to do harm to another would just do harm to me.

Another technique is to visualize the other person in my heart. I close my eyes, sit quietly, and watch my heart open and make room for a smaller version of that person. When feelings of anger arise, I gently place them in my heart where they are surrounded by love, good feelings and forgiveness. I often have to do this exercise several times in order to shift my thinking.

These are powerful visualizations that have worked for me. I'll bet there's a version of one of these that would work for you. It's worth it to change your mind about forgiveness if you need to. It's not a weakness to forgive but a fortifying action of acceptance and love. While I mourn the loss of lives and injury in the Boston marathon bombing, this situation offers me an excellent opportunity to practice unconditional forgiveness.

The book *Unconditional Forgiveness*, by Mary Hayes Grieco, is one I've been using to look at my forgiveness practice. I highly recommend it as a powerful tool to work through the process of forgiveness, especially for those stubborn situations where letting go of anger and hurt is more difficult.

As senior citizens, we are role models for our families and our community. We are looked to for good behavior, open thinking, acceptance and a non-judgmental mentality. Forgiving is a cornerstone of being in the world and a valuable asset that will bring you and others comfort and joy.

What Causes Senior Moments?

It's normal to experience some memory loss as we age, due to decreases in neurotransmitters or chemicals that communicate information throughout our brain and body. Usually these kinds of changes don't affect daily functioning or the ability to live independently, though in people who experience Alzheimer's disease, these decreases are significant and injurious to brain function.

People of all ages experience occasional memory loss. We refer to these lapses as senior moments, brain farts or spacing out. We joke about it, but the humor helps mask our terror when we enter a room and forget what we were going to do there, or when we pay for a purchase and leave the store without the item we just bought. I've been there, done that!

The brain uses forgetfulness as a way to avoid confusion and inhibit cognitive overload. It is selective, remembering important information and setting aside that which is less useful. Viewed from this perspective, forgetfulness is beneficial and a sign of proper brain functioning. But why do we experience these kinds of lapses at all?

There are many reasons for experiencing a blank in memory. Senior moments can be due to fatigue, stress, medication, or even multi-tasking. It is reported that anemia and thyroid disease can also affect temporary memory loss.

But I'm not stressed or tired, so what's my excuse? As long as the lapse is occasional and not due to a debilitating condition, my answer to this question is, "Lighten up." One episode of forgetfulness and we're ready to schedule an MRI! My tendency is to joke about it when I'm with others, but the less fuss I make about it, the faster I remember what I was going to do or say.

I have a few tips to reduce the incidence of senior moments if they're bothering you:

- Do one thing at a time.
- Get enough sleep and maintain a healthy diet.
- If you're stressed, develop stress management techniques.
- Reduce the need to multi-task.
- Quit relying on just your memory, and use some of those excellent electronics that keep track of dates and act as digital assistants.
- Replay memories in your mind to reinforce them.
- When trying to commit something to memory, use all your senses. Notice how things smell and feel, as well as how they look.

We can learn life lessons from senior moments. Let's experience as many of them as we need in order to receive the message that we should slow down and smell the roses. Let's not be embarrassed when we do something silly, like trying to remember where we parked the car at the mall.

Let's create a place where we have the luxury to do

one thing at a time. For those of us who are retired, we're done being show-offs, multi-tasking our little hearts out and proving that we can manage a myriad of tasks simultaneously. There's a bigger prize awaiting us when we slow down and focus, and that prize is joy, the kind of joy that shows up when we look out into the world and really see something different than we saw before.

Think of a memory lapse as a gift, a pause to take a break and enjoy what's happening around you, a reminder to be present in the moment.

Senior Moments
Aren't Just For Seniors

While sorting out the garage, a man spent ten minutes looking for a tie-wrap in order to tie a bunch of tie-wraps together.

A woman making chicken soup simmered the carcass and vegetables for several hours. When it was fragrant and tasty, she strained the broth, pouring the liquid down the sink. Then she stood there for five minutes, staring at the bones and trying to remember what the next step in soup-making was.

Sam went to a gas station to fill up his car. He normally paid with his debit card, but this time he actually had cash. He walked to the cashier and gave the man $10. Sam then walked back to his car, got inside, and drove away. Several minutes later, already on the highway, he realized he hadn't actually pumped any gas. Sam was too ashamed to go back.

A woman went to her bank to make a deposit. The teller-in-training couldn't find the account. The woman began to get irritated. "I always seem to get the trainees," she thought. She asked them to search by her name. Still nothing. Suddenly she realized she was at the wrong bank.

I can relate to these stories. Though none of these hilarious incidents happened to senior citizens, more often than not we characterize them as "senior moments."

Regardless of age, anyone can experience the momentary memory lapses we laughingly call "senior moments" or "brain farts." Distractions of all types can cause momentary memory lapses, whether it's traffic, a crying baby or trying to do too many things at once. Have you ever walked into another room only to forget why you went there in the first place? It makes us feel crazy, but it happens to everyone, not just seniors.

Our fast-paced society increases the chances of having senior moments. Multitasking makes it more difficult to retain thoughts because we don't give any one piece of information our undivided attention. Also, fatigue and stress that many of us experience because we're overworked reduce our ability to concentrate and focus on details. So it's not all about being older.

I don't mean to make light of this issue, but I do want to explain that senior citizens don't have the memory-loss market all to themselves. We should certainly find a better term for memory lapses than "senior moments." Having said that, however, anyone over 65 who experiences significant and continuing memory loss should contact their physician.

Are You Better Now?

There are some things I could do when I was younger that I cannot do now, like drive across the country by myself or retrieve something from a bottom shelf without using the counter to pull myself back up. But there are things I can do now that I could not do when I was younger, like keeping my mouth shut when I feel like telling someone, "You're wrong!" or getting the chores done before diving into something pleasurable.

I can now sit at a stoplight—a long stoplight—and not drum my fingers on the steering wheel or pick up my cell phone to check everyone's status (which is not only stupid but illegal in California). Now I can think of helping someone else before helping myself. I can even be the last one in the buffet line.

There is no definite way to determine if you are better now than before because the word *better* is so subjective and the concept is difficult to determine quantitatively. However, here are some guidelines I used to compare being better today with than when I was younger:

- How much time can I spend alone while enjoying every moment of it?
- How much fun can I have with the least amount of money?
- How large is my base of friends? I'm referring here to the kind of friends who will not only party with me but who will accompany me to my colonoscopy and settle me in at home when it is done. (Insert your own medical scenario here!)
- How connected do I feel to a strong spiritual community that engages, supports and educates me?
- How often do I give back, either materially or emotionally?

You can see how subjective it can be to determine precisely how much better you are now compared to 20, 30 or 40 years ago. I can tell even without having to answer each of the above questions. It's a feeling, an overall sense of well-being that permeates every part of my life. This doesn't mean my life is perfect, without hassles or mistakes or drama. It just means those problems don't define my happiness or my ability to be the person I want to be. That is another way I know I'm better now than before.

Stop and think of what you can do now that you couldn't do before, and vice versa. Based on your experience, is there specific advice you might share with younger people about improving their lives now?

Thanks for the Memory

I think of the human brain as a Library of Congress. The amount of information we encounter every day of our lives is overwhelming. There's no way to actually know all that you know. Conversely, there's a ton of stuff we can't seem to remember. I'm sure I've forgotten a library's worth of information, be it important, entertaining or nostalgic.

Why is it I can remember where I was the first time I heard the song "Louie, Louie" but I can't remember what I had for lunch yesterday? Why can't I remember the safe place I put that thing I wanted to be sure not to lose?

There exists a significant amount of scientific data to explain why we have trouble remembering things, but it can be pretty boring data. I know, however, that there are many fun and easy ways to improve your ability to remember more than you currently do, regardless of whether you're a senior citizen or a youngster, and I'll share a few of those in a moment.

Besides the practical reasons, there are a couple of psychological issues that might impact your ability to remember something. One of those is your attitude. Do you really *want* to remember?

A friend of mine needed help learning how to do certain tasks on his computer, and he'd have to be shown how to do these tasks every single time he wanted to do them. He was frustrated. Using a computer made him feel unqualified and not capable of doing the simplest of tasks. He kept throwing his hands up in despair and ultimately opted for a different, less electronic way to accomplish his task. While he said he couldn't remember what I'd repeatedly shown him, in truth he didn't see the value of doing this task on the computer to begin with. Be sure to ask yourself: How important is it for me to remember this? Do I really want to remember this?

Another question I ask is: *Who* is telling me to remember? If it's a grouchy spouse or the ghost of a crabby teacher or parent, there is a good chance you won't let whatever it is really sink in enough to remember it. However, the opposite might be true as well: the experience may have been so unpleasant you'll never forget it! You'll be able to tell the difference.

It's proven that reducing stress, eating a healthy diet, playing stimulating games and getting sufficient sleep all contribute to your ability to remember things. Here are a few other suggestions for exercising your memory muscle that you might not be aware of. Some may seem a bit off the wall, but different things work for different people, so hold your judgment.

- Sniff sprigs of rosemary or rosemary oil. Rosemary contains eucalyptol which stimulates memory.

- Laugh. Laughter is cerebral exercise; it cleans out the cobwebs and stimulates all parts of the brain, not just those related with specific activities.

- Get a grip. Clench your *right* fist right before you want to remember something, and then clench your *left* fist when you need to recall it.

- Spell it. Create acronyms for tasks you want to remember. One of mine is, "KPS" for "keys, phone, sunglasses."

- To remember someone's name, picture their name written across their forehead when you meet them.

- When you wake up in the morning, move your eyes from side to side for thirty seconds. This will align the two parts of your brain and cause your memory to work more smoothly.

- Say things you want to remember out loud.

I hope you'll find one or more of these memory tips useful. After all, who doesn't want to improve their memory? It's not just seniors who forget things. Like everything else, use it or lose it!

19
ZZZZZZZZZzzzzzzzzzzzzz

Do you nap? How do you feel about napping? Do you experience guilt when you do it? If you nap, how, when, where and for how long do you do it?

When I close my eyes I can still recall the feel of the hard cement floor under my thin mat at kindergarten during nap time. Ahhhh, nap time. I'd fight it for a nanosecond, but because I'd played so hard I couldn't help drifting off with visions of the coconut cookie and juice I'd get when I woke.

As an adult, however, I never napped because I thought it meant weakness, as if you couldn't get through your day without resting…like a child. But my opinions and habits about this delicious "sport" have changed.

I asked my friends how they felt about naps and was surprised to learn that many did indeed imbibe and felt no guilt about it whatsoever. By briefly dropping off the edge of consciousness in the middle of the day, many were able to steal the extra time needed to tackle tasks, either mental or physical. But what kind of naps and how long? While I conducted no formal survey, it seems the most popular naps were short, lasting ten minutes to half an hour, either sitting or lying down.

So I did an experiment. Because it takes me ten minutes to a half hour to fall asleep in the first place, I began by setting aside one hour for a nap. I found it easy to let drowsiness overcome me after lunch, especially if I picked up a book. When my eyelids felt heavy and I found myself re-reading the same paragraph multiple times for comprehension, I knew it was time.

I hadn't been lying down for five minutes when my cat, Kali, thought it would be fun to join me. Her warm body against mine kept me from tossing and turning, and, sure enough, I fell asleep. My internal clock wasn't used to this mid-day snooze, however, and I woke at 4:30 p.m., nearly two and a half hours later. Yikes!

Since that first nap experiment I've played around with times and places to hone my snoozing skills. While it appears the kindergarten nap has grown up, it's still my goal to keep it short. I suppose I'll just have to practice, practice, practice.

And the guilt? The scientific approach to perfecting this sport is keeping all guilt at bay. People in Latin countries as well as most European countries consider you odd if you *don't* indulge in the sacred, post-lunch, digestive ritual known as the *siesta*.

So join me! Kick off your shoes, close the shutters or lock your office door or put the sun shade on your car dash to reduce the amount of light, and let your internal monitor default to screen-saver mode. Visualize your body sinking into warm sand as your mind drifts off into a much needed mini-vacation.

Fear of Death

The sunnier side of my personality—and probably the more private side—told me not to write about my fear of death. It's so depressing. Who wants to think about that?

Awhile back I noticed that I was thinking more about death. In fact, every day. I couldn't figure it out since no one near me had died recently and I wasn't aware of any sense of foreboding. Where was this coming from? I looked inside myself and, at the same time, hit the books. I'm all about research when I have unanswered questions!

This chapter is my initial foray into the subject. My thoughts are open ended; I have no definitive conclusions, no neatly-wrapped-up-and-tied-with-a-bow outcomes. This is an opening to a conversation. If it's a conversation you want to have, great. If not, that's okay too.

I began by identifying ways to alleviate this fear of death—exercises I could do, ways to trick myself into accepting this scary thing that has lately been clouding my view of the world. I used an excellent book, *Who Dies?* by Stephen and Ondrea Levine, to guide my tentative journey.

One of the first things I learned was that part of my fear is due to lack of control. The impermanence of life can be rattling. I have worked so hard to set up a satisfying life that it seems almost insulting to have it end at some point without my input.

In *Who Dies?* the authors say that because we identify so much with our ideas, beliefs and possessions, we see death as losing who we are. We use everything we have to become someone or something—"I am..."— and death takes that away. If instead we step into the space of being whole, moving closer toward a state of openness about who and what we are, we are more inclined to see ourselves as the path instead of the scary thing at the end of the path. But it isn't an easy or linear conversation.

Staying open is challenging. The daily routine makes it difficult. Getting things done and taking care of business makes it challenging. One thing in our favor is that it gets easier to be more open as we age. We have more time to open wider by meditating, listening rather than talking, not rushing to judgment, and by choosing our battles. Things fall away as we age: friends, material things, and hopefully our anger about life's ultimate conclusion. It simply feels more comfortable and positive to be open to death, which will eventually affect all of us.

The truth is that we are so much more than our possessions or activities or self-image. If I can't see or touch something, it's easy for me to forget about it. I am grateful that my spiritual education, which expands my point of view, helps me know and trust that Universal love exists and that I am more than who I think I am. This knowledge allows me to free myself from the idea that I'm going to have to let go of a lot of "stuff" when I die. I may not want to let go, but I can feel better about letting go when I think of all that stuff being replaced with things like unconditional freedom, love, kindness, joy.

I wonder if I'm too obsessed, if I think about death too much, and I wonder if there are other people like me who carry it heavily through life until it's right in front of their face. I don't want to avoid things I could do now to make my life and my passing even better.

I've cracked open the door ever so slightly on this subject for myself and perhaps for you. There is a lot to explore about our attitudes and actions surrounding death. The more we do this, the less afraid we become to open that door a little wider.

Doing Nothing Does Everything

Once a month I have a No Tech Day. During this 24-hour period, I don't turn on my computer or my cell phone. I don't drive my car or watch TV, Netflix or videos, and I don't listen to music. I don't text, Tweet or use my landline. I don't microwave or do laundry. I will, however, turn on the heater if necessary and the lights in the evening. This day is a fasting of sorts, and it revitalizes me so that I can be more productive in the days that follow.

At church, my metaphysical abode, I have learned to practice silence and retreat. We've explored the value of spending time in silence and how to make that happen. If you've never taken a whole day to be alone or if you can't go for an hour without checking your computer or phone, you might benefit from a No Tech Day.

What do I do with myself during my No Tech Day? I sit in silence, I walk, I read, I feel the sun on my body as I contemplate my garden, and I meditate. I visit with friends if I have an appointment planned. I play with my cat, Kali, who seems to love these days when I have ample time to entertain her with cat toys or strings. I eat salads, but I miss having my morning coffee. I remind myself, though, that it's only for 24 hours.

Like many people, I can become overwhelmed by the fast-paced world of this powerful technology that, for the most part, enhances the way we live. We communicate, problem solve, create new ideas and develop systems at breakneck speed. We have trained ourselves to think on our feet, to multi-task and to make decisions on the fly instead of mulling over our reactions and responses in contemplative repose.

One reward of taking a break from a fast-paced life is being reminded how the simplicity of a quiet day enhances my appreciation of all that surrounds me. On a No Tech Day, I meditate several times, usually upon waking and again later in the day, sometimes leading to a delicious nap. I remember what silence sounds like, I become aware of the ambient sound all around me, and I stop to smell the flowers, both literally and metaphorically. I need these retreat days to bring me back in touch with the simple things in life.

No Tech Days may appear effortless, but they can be challenging to pull off if you've never gone without electronics for 24 hours. You can do it, and you will improve the more often you do it. Try it for an hour at a time at first, and don't get discouraged. I promise you it'll be worth it.

Be the Best "I" You Can Be

You are many things to many people in this world. You are a parent, sibling, student, teacher, friend, lover. But you are only you to yourself. No one will ever fully appreciate all your idiosyncrasies and foibles as much as you do.

We don't have time to waste on things that are out of our control, things that don't bring us joy, things that deplete us of the love and compassion we require to grow and expand. Life isn't a dress rehearsal; it is opening night!

I recently took a long, hard look at what moves,

incites and enrages me in my life. What is important enough to speak up for and not compromise on? I realized that I wanted to:

- stare at the brilliant ocean waves crashing on the beach, memorizing the glaring white foam;
- inhale the sweet scent of the folds of a precious baby's neck;
- take a mental snapshot when Kali twists her head back from my lap to stare lovingly into my eyes;
- listen for the umpteenth time to that piece of classical music that makes me swoon;
- feel the soothing caress of comfort from a friend or loved one;
- recreate the event or retell the story that made me laugh so hard I nearly cried.

This is my list today, but it will probably change in the future. That's okay, because it is not the list so much as the process of being the best "I" can be.

A No-Cost Way to
Improve Your Life

Wayne Dyer and Oprah Winfrey have both expounded on the subject of abundance over the years. Well-known and respected authors have written tomes about abundance and its role in life. Within my own spiritual community, abundance is taught as a cornerstone of a joyous life.

Acknowledging the abundance around us is a powerful and no-cost way to improve your life. I'm all for inexpensive ways to improve my life, and I never get tired of being reminded of the goodness that comes from creating prosperity and celebrating all the abundance that already exists.

The practice of abundance helps mold a positive and upbeat lifestyle. With pervasive reports of crime, destruction, poor economic forecasts, and war, to name a few pessimistic talking points, it's quite easy to wallow in the negative despite all the wonderment in the Universe. Yet you've got an uphill battle before you if you focus on negative issues when all around you is the beauty of life.

Just watch the evening news every night for a week. We're bombarded with messages that say things aren't good out there, and if they are good it's only temporary. There will inevitably be a shooting, tornado, financial crisis or political scandal to rob you of the true joys in life.

What does abundance look like? When I think of abundance, I don't focus on what I want. I think about what I already have. And that doesn't change with the stock market, the weather or with what so-and-so said about me to someone else. But many people define abundance as freedom, happiness, health, love, peace.

You have to live an authentic life to have an abundant life. Abundance is not about what possessions you have but rather what you truly believe about your possessions and attitudes that comprise your life. You can't truly believe in lack, want, violence, and at the same time believe that there is enough in the world to meet all your needs. You have to let go of the negative to allow room for the positive to enter your soul.

The next time you find yourself explaining all that you're grateful for, toss in a few affirmations about the abundance you currently have in your life. Celebrate and declare all the abundance that you have manifested. It's your choice. Choose abundance, choose the celebration of all there is, and choose the affirmation of all that the Universe currently provides for you.

24
Cringe-worthy E-Mail

I'm on many e-mail lists and receive regular missives about upcoming social and civic activities. When General Foods refuses to label GMOs in its products, I get an e-mail, a call to action. When a particular political party throws a roadblock in the path of progress or hinders positive change, I get e-mail asking me to sign petitions, write letters or share a point of view with my Facebook friends. I even have an app on my phone that allows me to scan the purchase tags of items to find out if that company has ever supported apartheid or been associated with controversial activities like having its products made in sweatshops.

I appreciate having this information so effortlessly at my disposal and value my participation in many of these causes. Naturally I'm going to stand up and acknowledge that I want a government shutdown to end. Of course I'm going to say I abhor underage workers slaving away in unhealthy work environments for pennies a day. It's what happens to me *after* I take these stands that often leaves a toxic feeling in my soul.

The more I became involved and enlightened, the more my mailbox becomes filled with negative messages of what is wrong in the world—criminals, corrupt politicians, unethical companies, the environment with its problems of global warming and shockingly aberrant weather in the form of storms like Hurricane Sandy or super typhoons in the Philippines.

I sometimes cringe when I log on each morning, afraid to see what terrible event or person was plotting to ruin the world. It can cause me to feel nervous, afraid, naïve, or pessimistic about being able to find a safe place to spend my day.

Some people can acknowledge this daily barrage and let it pass right through them, but not me. It burrows into my heart and threatens my practice of living and loving fully each day. It beats me down more than I'd like to admit. But I have determination!

So I began a new regime and unsubscribed from all those organizations that are certainly trying to do good things in the world but are upsetting my outlook with their notifications. While this purge won't entirely solve the build-up of negative input, and though I know it will accumulate again, I feel relieved.

This process reminds me that I'm in control of my happiness regardless of what is happening out there and regardless of what I believe I should be doing about it. My well-being is tied to a good and generous world that supports fellowship and love, and I have to choose activities which reflect that attitude.

I cannot be a target for the negative and then turn around and project the positive. This doesn't mean I give up understanding global issues and supporting good causes. It means I periodically need to step back and reclaim my peace and prosperity in order to more fully live a well-rounded life.

The Icing or the Cake?

I was talking to Nancy recently, the 40-year-old daughter of a friend. Nancy is a woman beginning the process to end her second marriage. She is creative and smart and independent and she has always supported herself. She likes men who give her lots of freedom, time and space to pursue not only her work but her hobbies as well, which include singing and garden landscaping.

In our conversation, Nancy was lamenting the fact that she had yet again found herself in a relationship with a man who claimed that she is his entire reason for being. He said the only thing he wanted to do is help her, and that his joy was in supporting her and making life easy for her. What he was saying, in fact, was that Nancy was his cake.

In the vernacular, "cake" signifies the main deal. It's the core of a person—their ability to be creative, to grow, to be happy with themselves. It's the thing we look to within in order to survive in the world.

You can't be someone else's cake because that means they put you ahead of themselves, which puts pressure on you to be and do for them, which is not healthy for either of you.

While you can't be someone's cake, you can be their icing. Icing makes everything better. It's returning home after a long day and being excited that the other person is there. It's having someone to share troubles and difficulties with, knowing that the person won't judge you and will listen attentively and strive to see your point of view. It's going to a party, an event or vacation and having the experience enhanced by that person's presence.

Nancy feels suffocated and tied down and responsible for the happiness of her partner. She feels like a delicate butterfly who wants to experience all the world has to offer but is being restrained by an ever-tightening grip of a partner who needs her to define him.

Trying to be someone's cake is suffocating and unhealthy. Being the icing is joyous and exciting and uplifting for all involved. It gives space and freedom for both parties to grow and enrich their own cake. Nancy has lots of work to do around her choices in relationships, yet we can all learn her lesson about cake and icing. Do you allow your partner, child, friend to be their own cake? Do you demand to be a part of that cake, or do you simply want to share your icing?

21st Century Communication

"You never call. You never write." To this maxim you can now add, "You never e-mail. You never Tweet." So we wade into the electronic waters to try and stay relevant. But when learning and using new forms of communication, we must understand the guidelines of communicating that go along with them.

Communication has changed significantly in the last several years. It's easy and effective to communicate if you're standing in front of the person. You speak and use hand gestures, facial expressions and intonation to get your point across. "I don't think so" can be a straightforward response to a question, a flip remark to a comical situation, or a sharp retort to a perceived injustice. The meaning is discerned by all the information that accompanies the words.

I remember writing thank-you notes with fountain pens and Eaton stationary. After Christmas and birthdays, I was required to write these expressions of gratitude to grandmothers and other relatives. I hated writing them, but I loved receiving them when I was the gift giver. I have friends who have taken the Thank You note to an art form and send them out for myriad reasons, including dinners and parties. As much as I enjoy finding missives in my mailbox, I do tell my relatives that I am fine with an email Thank You from their young kids to acknowledge that they received my gift.

I once attended a Senior Expo where I shared information about my blog, Antonia's Senior Moments. To read a blog, one must obviously have access to the Internet and be savvy enough to navigate it. Before the event, I wondered what percentage of seniors who came by my table would claim, proudly or otherwise, a complete lack of interest and even disdain for all things computer-related. I thought it might be 50-50. But I was wrong.

The majority of seniors I spoke with that day embrace, to various degrees, electronic forms of communication. Some told me they squeak by just using e-mail, and others said they are also active on Facebook, Twitter and more. A few seniors stay as far away from the Internet as possible, not even dipping a toe into e-mail, a fact which frustrates friends and family who routinely rely on electronic mail to connect and exchange information with them.

Over the years, new protocol has been developed when using various forms of electronic communication. Some people refer to them as rules, but I think of them as suggestions or guidelines. You won't be dropped from the social registry for doing things incorrectly in the e-communication world, but you may send the wrong message to your audience if you don't understand the main guidelines.

First, always remember that communication typed via e-mail, Twitter, or text messages doesn't include all those wonderful and, yes, sometimes irritating body and facial gestures that complement the meaning of the spoken word. Written messages are flat words, and their meaning, without gestures, facial expressions or vocal intonation, can be misread.

Be careful using humor and sarcasm. Arguments can start and feelings may be hurt when words are misinterpreted by the recipient. Reserve any communications that might be open to misunderstanding for face-to-face meetings when possible. Never use e-mail or other electronic messaging to communicate something that would be better relayed in person. Confrontation can be uncomfortable, but avoid the tendency to hide behind your impersonal keyboard. Just don't do it. It can be rude, hurtful, and confusing. I've learned this the hard way.

Other suggestions for positive electronic communication:

- TYPING IN ALL CAPS IS THE SAME AS SHOUTING and is considered annoying.

- Some people think it acceptable to forego proper

grammar and capitalization in e-communications. While I may not always start my e-mails with "Dear So and So," I do think it imperative to use correct grammar and punctuation throughout.

- Include a subject line to let the reader know what the following message is about.

- Keep it short and simple. Reread your message before sending and delete any unnecessary verbiage.

- Always Spell Check.

A personal pet peeve is receiving e-mail that has been forwarded from the sender's brother's niece's secretary's father. This amasses so many addresses and messages of the previous receivers that I have to wade through before I get to the cartoon, joke or kitty montage that was meant for me. You can delete the forwarded messages and e-mail addresses before you resend it to your crowd. Deleting all the previous addresses and comments makes the receiver feel like you intended the message just for them.

I am aware that electronic communication can be intimidating and confusing for those who have spent the majority of their lives with more personal interactions. Sometimes, rather than learning the correct way to use electronic communication, we plunge ahead and plead ignorance when we screw up. I encourage you, however, to take the time to learn the proper ways to communicate using electronic devices. I guarantee it'll pay off in terms of being heard and getting your meaning across to your audience, even if that audience includes people much younger than you.

ANTONIA ALBANY has written about aging issues for several years in blog posts and her latest book entitled *Golden Grace: Embracing the Richness of Our Later Years*. She shares her humorous, spiritual and practical views on making the most of our senior years in this book and at her website, TheJoyOfAgingGratefully.com.

She lives in the wine country of northern California with her husband and cat and is available for public speaking engagements.